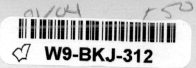

Beginning
to Heal

Also by the authors

The Courage to Heal

and by Ellen Bass

I Never Told Anyone: Writings by Women Survivors of Child Sexual Abuse (coeditor)

I Like You to Make Jokes with Me, But I Don't Want You to Touch Me (for children)

Our Stunning Harvest (poetry)

For Earthly Survival (poetry)

I'm Not Your Laughing Daughter (poetry)

and by Laura Davis

The Courage to Heal Workbook

Allies in Healing: When the Person You Love Was Sexually Abused as a Child

Beginning to Heal

A First Book for Survivors of Child Sexual Abuse

Ellen Bass and Laura Davis

HarperPerennial

A Division of HarperCollins*Publishers*

Ellen Bass offers lectures for survivors and their supporters and training seminars for counselors. For a schedule of upcoming events, please write to the address below.

The authors welcome any feedback or responses to *Beginning to Heal* but regret that they are unable to answer individual letters.
Ellen Bass and Laura Davis
P.O. Box 5296
Santa Cruz, CA 95063-5296

BEGINNING TO HEAL. Copyright © 1993 by Ellen Bass and Laura Davis. All rights reserved. Printed in the United States of America. No part of this book may be used or reproduced in any manner whatsoever without written permission except in the case of brief quotations embodied in critical articles and reviews. For information address HarperCollins Publishers, Inc., 10 East 53rd Street, New York, NY 10022.

HarperCollins books may be purchased for educational, business, or sales promotional use. For information write Special Markets Department, HarperCollins Publishers, Inc., 10 East 53rd Street, New York, NY 10022.

FIRST EDITION

Designed by Laura Hough Design

Library of Congress Cataloging-in-Publication Data

Bass, Ellen.
   Beginning to heal : a first book for survivors of child sexual abuse / Ellen Bass, Laura Davis.
      p.   cm.
   ISBN 0-06-096927-X (pbk.)
   1. Adult child sexual abuse victims—United States—Psychology. 2. Abused women—United States—Psychology. 3. Child molesting—United States. I. Title
HV6570.2.B37 1993
362.7'64'0973—dc20   92-54425

02 03 04 05   ❖/HC   14 15 16 17 18 19 20

"Don't run away from it. Don't bury it. Don't try to produce a different reality getting all strung out on something, or eating your way through the feelings. Don't slash your wrists. Just deal with it, because it's going to keep coming back if you continue living anyway. It's painful, but it's just part of life, really."

— Soledad, 28-year-old survivor

"There's more than anger, more than sadness, more than terror. There's hope."

— Edith Horning, 46-year-old survivor

"Don't give up. That's the best thing I could tell somebody who just remembered she was a survivor. There are people who have lived through it, and as trite and stupid as it sounds to you right now, you will not be in so much pain later. If you made it this far, you've got some pretty good stuff in you. *Don't give up on yourself.*"

— Catherine, 35-year-old survivor

Contents

Acknowledgments

With deep appreciation, we thank all the survivors who so generously shared their stories with us.

We'd like to acknowledge Seal Press and authors Ginny NiCarthy and Sue Davidson for their book for battered women, *You Can Be Free: An Easy-to-Read Handbook for Abused Women,* which inspired *Beginning to Heal.*

We'd also like to thank Marilyn Boutwell of Literacy Volunteers of America for reviewing this manuscript and offering valuable guidance. And we thank Stephanie Smith and reading specialists Elsie Staley and Karyn Bristol for their helpful advice and suggestions.

And as always, we are grateful for the intelligence and vision of our editor, Janet Goldstein, and the enthusiasm and skill of our agent, Charlotte Raymond.

A LETTER TO OUR READERS

Dear Reader:

We wrote *Beginning to Heal* for people who are just starting to look at the issue of sexual abuse in their lives. The stories and examples in the book are about women, but men who've been sexually abused should feel free to use this book too.

Beginning to Heal will let you know you're not alone and that there is a way out of the pain you're feeling. As you read, you may feel great relief. You may feel proud, strong, or able to make positive changes in your life.

But you may also feel afraid, angry, or deeply sad. If you have unfamiliar or upsetting feelings as you read, don't be alarmed. Strong feelings are part of healing.

If you don't have any feelings at all, that may mean you're not feeling safe enough yet to face the pain. That's okay. Take your time.

Reading this book is a little like healing itself. You don't go in a straight line, from beginning to end. Instead, you can go at your own pace, in your own way. You can skip chapters if you want to. Or read a page more than once.

If you come to a part of this book that's hard for you, you don't have to grit your teeth and keep reading. It's okay to stop, take a break, talk to someone for support, and come back to it later.

This is your book. You can use it in any way that's helpful to you.

We wish you courage and support on your healing journey.

Ellen Bass & *Laura Davis*

P.S. *Beginning to Heal* is drawn from our longer book, *The Courage to Heal*. We've made this book shorter and easier to read so more people can use it. When you're ready for a more thorough guide to healing, *The Courage to Heal* can offer further support.

Part One

The Healing Process

Healing Is Possible

"There's nothing as wonderful as starting to heal, waking up in the morning and knowing that nobody can hurt you if you don't let them."

If you have been sexually abused, you are not alone. One out of three girls and one out of seven boys are abused by the time they reach eighteen. Sexually abused children come from every race, religion, and culture. They come from rich families and poor families. Abusers can be men or women, family members, friends, neighbors, teachers, counselors, priests, babysitters, and strangers.

If you were abused as a child, you are probably still dealing with the effects in your life today. You may be having trouble at school, on your job, with relationships and sex, or in your family. You may feel bad about yourself or think something is wrong with you. These problems, and many others, can be connected to the abuse you experienced while you were growing up.

The most important thing for you to know is that it is possible to heal from child sexual abuse. You don't have to live with the effects of abuse for the rest of your life. If you are willing to work hard and find good support, you can not only heal but thrive.

If you have been sexually abused,
you are not alone.

Was I Abused?

You've probably heard a lot about sexual abuse, but you may not be sure if your experience fits the definition.

Think back to when you were growing up. Did any of these things happen to you?

- Were you ever touched unnecessarily in your private parts?
- Were you forced to touch someone else's private parts?
- Were you made to pose for sexual pictures?
- Were you forced to have oral sex?
- Were you raped or did you have things forced inside your vagina or anus?
- Were you fondled or kissed in a way that felt bad to you?
- Were you forced to watch people have sex?
- Were you shown sexual movies?
- Were you forced to have enemas, genital exams, or

other medical procedures that weren't really needed?
- Were you told you were only good for sex?
- Were you ridiculed about your body or your sexuality?
- Were you pressured into having sex you didn't really want?
- Were you involved in selling your body for sex?
- Were you forced to abuse or hurt someone else?
- Were you forced to take part in rituals that involved violence, sex, or torture?

If any of these things happened to you, then you were sexually abused.

Does My Experience Really Count?

As you think about your past, you may clearly remember what happened to you. But sometimes memories are fuzzy or unclear. Memories can also be blocked out completely as a way of coping with the pain.

Sometimes survivors think that what happened to them isn't bad enough to qualify as abuse. They say things like, "It wasn't incest—he was just a friend of the family," or "It only happened once," or "It was just my brother and he was only a year older than me." But your pain counts.

The fact that someone else has suffered from abuse that was worse than yours does not take away your suffering. The important thing in defining abuse is not the physical act that took place. It's how you felt as a child. An abuser used power to manipulate and control you. Your trust was shattered and the world stopped being safe. You felt terrified, hurt, ashamed, or confused.

Even abuse that isn't physical can leave deep scars. Your father treated you like you were his wife instead of his daughter. Your uncle walked naked around the house making comments about your body. These acts, though not directly physical, hurt you.

It doesn't matter how often you were abused. A mother can stick her hand in her daughter's underwear in thirty seconds. After that the world is not the same.

The Healing Process

This book is about the healing process. Healing begins when you recognize that you were abused. And it leads to the satisfying experience we call *thriving*.

If you are willing to work hard and find good support, you can not only heal but thrive.

Survivors have taught us that there are recognizable stages in the healing process. This book will give you a map so you can see where you are, what you've already done, and what still lies ahead.

We've presented the stages of healing in a particular order, but you may not experience them that way. You may spend time focusing intensely on the abuse. Then your attention may shift more to your current life. When something in your life changes—you start a relationship, leave home, or have a child—you may deal with the abuse again, from a new point of view. Each time, you learn more, feel more, and make more lasting changes.

This book will give you a map of the healing process, so you can see where you are, what you've already done, and what still lies ahead.

The further along you are in the healing process, the more you'll be able to take care of yourself along the way. You'll be able to laugh, to experience pleasure along with the pain. You won't change your history, but it will no longer seem like the most important thing in your life.

There is no clear end to the healing process. It's a way of growing that continues throughout your life.

You deserve this healing.

The Decision
to Heal

"This has given me the opportunity to look at me. It's not all bad. You do heal. And you do become stronger. I don't know what it would take to flatten me, but it would have to be something really big. I am, in fact, a survivor."

The decision to heal from child sexual abuse is a powerful, positive choice. It is a commitment every survivor deserves to make. Healing can bring to your life a richness and depth you never dreamed possible:

> "For the first time, I'm appreciating things like the birds and the flowers, the way the sun feels on my skin—you know, really simple things. I can read a good book. I can sit in the sun. I don't ever remember enjoying these things,

even as a little kid. I've woken up. If this hadn't happened, I'd still be asleep. So for the first time, I feel alive. And you know that's something to go for."

Survivors decide to heal for many different reasons. Some say they were "falling apart at the seams" or "hitting bottom." Others are motivated by changes in their lives. A young girl turns her stepfather in for molesting her and the judge sends her to therapy. A young woman finds herself unable to stay close to her boyfriend once they get married. A mother starts having terrible nightmares when her daughter reaches the age she was when the abuse began. An older woman quits drinking and starts having troubling memories from childhood.

The decision to heal from child sexual abuse is a powerful, positive choice.

What Is It Like to Heal?

Once you decide to face your abuse, you probably want to get it over with as quickly as possible. Unfortunately, healing doesn't work that way. Lasting change takes time.

It is always worth it to heal. But it is rarely easy. Deciding to heal can lead to serious conflicts with people you care about. You may find it hard to study, work, take care of your children, or even make dinner. You may be unable to sleep, eat, or simply stop crying:

"If I'd known anything could hurt this much or
be this sad, I never would have decided to heal.
And at the same time you can't go back. You
can't unremember."

There will probably be times when you wonder if
healing is worth the risk. But as one survivor put it, "Taking that risk was the most promising choice I had."

It is scary to face the unknown. But it is also a
tremendous relief to stop running away from the pain:

"There is comfort in knowing that you don't
have to pretend anymore, that you are going to
do everything within your power to heal."

---

*It is a tremendous relief to stop running away
from the pain.*

Don't Try to Do It Alone

You can't heal from child sexual abuse alone. You need
to break the silence that has surrounded the abuse and
reach out for support.

At least one person needs to know about your
pain and your healing. That person can be a friend,
counselor, spouse or partner, fellow survivor, or family
member. Hopefully, you will have many people who support you. But start with one. Find someone you trust and
talk about it.

The Emergency Stage

"I felt like I was standing in a room, looking at the floor. I was shattered all over it. I was picking up pieces of my life and looking at them, saying, 'Do I want to keep this? Is this of any use to me anymore? When will the pain stop?'"

Many survivors go through a period when sexual abuse is all they think about. You talk about it to anyone who will listen. You think about it all day and have nightmares at night. Your life is full of crises. You can't stop crying, and it's hard to function.

Women often describe the early stages of their healing as a natural disaster: "It was like being caught in an avalanche." "It was like an earthquake."

Here's how one woman, Catherine, experienced the emergency stage:

"It was like there were large six-foot-high letters in my living room every day when I woke up: **INCEST!** I felt everyone knew I was an incest victim. I thought I looked like one.

"I had no energy to deal with other people or their problems. My reserves had been drained. For a long time, all I cared about was going to sleep and being able to wake up the next day.

"I had to find people who would sit with me no matter how I felt. I had one friend who'd been beaten when she was a kid. She understood. I could call her when I felt horrible, and she'd let me come over to just eat and watch TV.

"I also had to find a safe place to be alone. I went for walks in the woods. I ran a lot. I'd go for twenty-mile bike rides.

"The only thing that saved me when I felt totally cut off was that I had my therapist's phone number written all over my house. I had it on the mirror in the bathroom. I had it in my journal. I had it in books I was reading. I burned it in my memory, so at any time I could call her. Many times, just making the call and getting her answering machine, and being able to leave a message in my cracking, crying voice, let me know I could reach out. I knew she would call me eventually, and I could hold out till then.

"After a year, I was able to lift my head up a little bit and notice that the season had changed. I started to realize that even though I was an incest survivor, I could go on with my life. That was a tremendous relief."

Surviving the Emergency Stage

The most important thing to remember about the emergency stage is that it will end. There will be a time when you will not be thinking about sexual abuse twenty-four hours a day. Until then, *your job is to take care of yourself and to keep yourself safe.*

- **Don't try to hurt or kill yourself.** (See the box on page 14.)

- **Remind yourself that you're not going crazy.** You're going through a natural part of the healing process.

- **Find people you can talk to.** And get support from other survivors.

- **Allow yourself to think about the abuse as much as you need to.**

- **Drop any responsibilities that aren't essential.**

- **Don't use alcohol or drugs to stop the pain.** Numbing your feelings will only make the crisis last longer.

- **Get out of dangerous or abusive situations.** If your husband is beating you, if your children are in danger, or if someone is still sexually abusing you, get the help you need to leave. Call the National Child Abuse Hotline at 1-800-422-4453.

- **Sit tight and ride out the storm.** Your thinking isn't that clear right now. Unless you're in danger, this is not usually a good time for major life changes.

- **Develop a belief in something greater than yourself.** Spirituality can give you hope and strength.

- **Talk to people who are farther along in their healing.**

- **Do as many nice things for yourself as possible.**

Don't Kill Yourself

Sometimes you feel so bad, you don't want to live. The pain is too great. You hate yourself and feel afraid. You want to die.

These are your real feelings. Don't deny them. *But don't act on them. Don't kill yourself.*

We have lost far too many survivors already. Too many victims—children, teenagers, and adults—have lacked support and hope, and out of despair, have killed themselves. We can't afford to lose you. You deserve to live.

Read the chapter on anger. You have been taught to turn your anger inward. When you feel so bad you want to die, you need to refocus your anger toward the people who hurt you. As you get in touch with your anger, your self-hate will lessen. You will want to live.

This takes time. Right now, get help. If the first person you call isn't helpful, try again. Make a list of support people and their phone numbers. If you start feeling like you want to hurt yourself, call them. If you don't know who to call, ask the operator for suicide prevention. A call to them can save your life.

You may feel like you can't stand it another minute. But the feelings will pass. You can learn to wait them out.

Each time you bear the pain of your feelings without hurting yourself, you become stronger. Each time you reach out for help, you defeat your abusers. You have not let them destroy you.

The most important thing to remember about the
emergency stage is that it will end. Until then,
your job is to take care of yourself and to
keep yourself safe.

Tips for Dealing with Panic

Panic is what you feel when your feelings seem out of
control. You're scared. Your heart is pounding. You can't
catch your breath. The fear keeps getting stronger. You
want to run away.

Panic attacks can be caused by triggers—things in
the present that remind you of times you were terrified in
the past.

Trying to push a memory away can also cause panic.

When you start to feel panicky, don't rush into
action. Don't drive. Don't drink or abuse drugs. Don't
hurt yourself or anyone else. Acting out of panic leads to
poor choices.

To calm yourself down, do whatever works for you.
When you're not feeling scared, make a list of things that
help you relax. The next time you panic, pick up your list
and do the thing at the top of the list. Then work your
way down.

Everyone's list will be different. But be sure you
include the phone numbers of people you can call. When
you're feeling scared, it's often the hardest time to reach
out. Do it anyway.

A sample list might look like this:

Things to Do in a Panic

1) Breathe.
2) Get my teddy bear.
3) Call Natalie.
4) Call Nona if Natalie's not home. Keep calling down my list of support people.
5) Stroke the cat.
6) Take a hot bath.
7) Write a hundred times, "I'm safe. They can't hurt me anymore."
8) Go for a run.
9) Listen to soothing music.
10) Pray.
11) Write in my journal for fifteen minutes without stopping.
12) Watch an old movie on TV.
13) Eat Campbell's tomato soup.
14) Start again at the top.

When you're feeling scared, it's often the hardest time to reach out. Do it anyway.

What Gives Me Hope

This is what some survivors told us:

"My friend Patricia gave me hope. She would basically talk me into wanting to live."

"The thing that gives me hope is remembering what my therapist kept saying to me, over and over, 'This is part of the change process.' I held on to that when there was really nothing else to hold on to."

"I was a nun in a contemplative order. Because I had lived that lifestyle, I knew things took a long time. I knew the process of becoming holy, of knowing God, was very slow. Day by day, I just knew I was growing closer to God. It was the same with the incest. I just trusted that something was happening, that there was a hidden growth going on."

"My sister inspires me through her struggle. She had it a lot worse than I did, and she is struggling to live."

"My own inner strength gives me hope. I just won't quit. Period."

_____

My own inner strength gives me hope. I just won't quit. Period.

_____

Remembering

"I've looked the memories in the face and smelled their breath. They can't hurt me anymore."

Many children cope with abuse by blocking it out and forgetting it. As a result, many survivors don't remember they were abused. Then something happens in their lives to trigger the memories. Ten, twenty, or forty years after the abuse, memories start to break through.

Remembering abuse "out of the blue" can make you feel crazy. It can be hard to take these memories seriously. You might ask yourself, "Where are they coming from? Am I losing my mind?"

Forgetting the abuse and then remembering it later is a survival tool that makes sense. You forget until it's safe enough to remember. Your mind protects you.

The fact that you're remembering now means you're ready to learn about your history. Often, a particular event or shift in your life brings up memories that have been buried for years.

Some of the common times people remember their abuse are:

- During puberty or a similar period of sexual awakening
- When the abuser or a family member dies
- When you quit drinking, using drugs, or stop another addiction
- When a relationship ends *or* becomes more committed
- When you get sick or have surgery
- During dental work or medical exams
- While making love, getting a massage, or using your body in a new way
- When you're the victim of a rape or attack
- When you read about abuse in the newspaper or hear about it on TV
- When a friend tells you his or her story of childhood abuse
- When a child you know is abused
- During pregnancy or childbirth
- When your child reaches the age you were when you were abused

Not all survivors forget their abuse. Many remember each incident but forget how it felt at the time:

> "I could rattle off the facts of my abuse like a grocery list, but remembering the fear and terror and pain was another matter entirely."

If this is true for you, remembering may mean uncovering the feelings you had as a child.

Forgetting the abuse and then remembering it later is a survival tool that makes sense.

What Remembering Is Like

The process of remembering is like putting a jigsaw puzzle together. Memories often come back in bits and pieces. They can seem like a dream, or as vivid as a snapshot:

> "I'd be driving home from my therapist's office and I'd start having flashes of things—like bloody sheets, or taking a bath, or throwing away my nightgown. For a long time, I remembered all the things around being raped but not the rape itself."

You may have flashbacks in which you relive experiences you had as a child. You smell the abuser's breath. You see the room you slept in as a child. You feel the terror you felt as a six-year-old.

Most of us expect memories to be visual. But they're not always that way. One woman was held face down on the seat of a car and raped by her father. She didn't *see* anything. But she heard him. And when she began to write about it in Spanish, her native language, it all came back.

You may also remember with your body. Your lover touches you and you feel disgusted. You can't stand being kissed in a particular place. You don't have specific pictures, but your body remembers the abuse.

You may also find yourself thinking differently about past events. When you were eleven, everyone called you Uncle Sam's girlfriend and you hated to sit on his lap. What was that really about?

Letting Memories In

In the beginning, you won't have control over when and how you remember. If you try to push the memories away, you may end up exhausted, plagued by headaches, panic attacks, or nightmares. It's best to just let the memories come through:

- **Find a place where you'll be safe.**
- **Call a support person if you want to be with someone.** Or you might prefer being alone.
- **Don't fight it.** Relax and let the memory come. Don't use drugs, alcohol, or food to push it down.
- **Remember, it's just a memory.** Your abuser is not really hurting you now, even if it feels that way. Reliving a memory is part of your healing. It's not more abuse.
- **Expect to have a response.** It's painful and draining to remember. It may take you a while to recover.

- **Nurture yourself.** You need extra comfort and care right now.
- **Tell at least one other person.** You suffered alone as a child. You don't have to do that again.

As you remember, it's important to let yourself feel. Yet that's very hard to do. When you remember the terror, the physical pain, and the panic, the feelings can be as intense as the actual experience:

> "I found myself slipping into the feelings I'd had during the abuse. There was this tremendous isolation. I got in touch with how frightening the world is. It was the worst of the fear finally coming up. I felt like it was right at the top of my neck all the time, ready to come out in a scream."

Having to experience the feelings is one of the hardest parts of remembering. Yet it can also bring relief:

> "The more I heal, the more I see these memories are literally stored in my body, and they've got to get out. Otherwise I'm going to carry them forever."

Reliving a memory is part of your healing. It's not more abuse.

"But I Don't Have Any Memories"

If you don't remember your abuse, you're not alone. Many survivors don't have memories, and some never get memories. This doesn't necessarily mean they weren't abused. And it doesn't stop them from healing. One survivor explained:

> "Do I want to know if something physical happened between my father and me? I think you have to be strong enough to know. Our minds are wonderful in the way they protect us. I think when I'm strong enough to know, I'll know.
>
> "I obsessed for a year trying to remember. Then I thought, 'Let's act as if.' It's like you come home and your home has been robbed. Everything has been thrown in the middle of the room. The window is open. The curtain is blowing in the wind. The cat is gone. You know somebody robbed you, but you're never going to know who. So what are you going to do? Sit there and try to figure it out while your stuff lies around? No, you start to clean it up. You put bars on the window. You *assume* someone was there.
>
> "That's how I acted. I had all the symptoms. I had to ask myself, 'Why would I be feeling all this if something didn't happen?' I'm left with the damage. What am I going to do? Wait twenty more years for a memory? I'd rather get better."

It's natural to want "proof" that you were abused. Yet the real proof is in the damage to your life. Even if you never get clear memories, you still can heal.

Even if you never get clear memories, you still can heal.

Believing It Happened

"Up until three months ago, I didn't *really* believe it happened. 'I only imagined it.' I was acting as if it happened. I'd go to an incest survivors' group. I'd freely tell people. But when I was alone, I'd say, 'Of course it didn't *really* happen.'"

To heal from child sexual abuse, you must believe that you were a victim. Yet this is hard to do. When children are abused, it becomes dangerous for them to trust their own perceptions. You couldn't admit that the same neighbor who taught you to ride a bike also made you touch his penis. That was just too horrible to bear. So you pretended it didn't happen.

Children will go to great lengths to deny their own perceptions:

"When my father would come into my room at night, I'd think, 'That's not my father. That's an alien being. Invaders have taken over his body.'"

If the adults around you told you that your experiences didn't happen, you probably became confused and unsure about what was real. Your brother said he was just tucking you in. Your stepfather told you it was for your own good. Your mother said you were dreaming. Your uncle said, "You're crazy. No one will ever believe you."

It's not just family members who deny abuse. Teachers, doctors, counselors, and ministers sometimes do, too. They say things like, "But your grandfather is a deacon in the church," or "You should be over that by now."

And of course, you don't want it to be true.

No wonder it's hard to believe in yourself.

On the other hand, you may have no trouble believing you were abused. You have a sibling who was there. A mother who says, "But honey, I had to stay with him." An abuser who admits it.

Yet even if your family insists that nothing ever happened, you can still trust your own experience. Even if your memories feel too extreme to be real or too unimportant to count, you have to come to terms with the fact that someone did those things to you.

The Role of Denial

One of the most common ways people deal with hurt is denial. We pretend it never happened. But to heal, we have to face the truth.

One of the most common ways people deal with hurt is denial. We pretend it never happened.

You also need to be with people who believe and support you:

> "I would talk to my therapist about what people had done to me in my family. And she would say to me, 'That's abuse. It's terrible that happened to you.' And I was shocked, because I thought I had a normal childhood. My first year and a half was spent just accepting the fact that I had been abused."

Even once you know the facts are true, you may still have trouble believing it happened. It takes time for the knowledge to really sink in. Eventually, your belief will grow stronger.

To heal, you have to face the truth.

Breaking Silence

"You know how they say, 'Speak the truth and the truth shall set you free.' Well, that's how it really is. I'm not in a cage anymore. There are no more secrets. And it's the secrets that kill you."

To heal from child sexual abuse, you need to tell the truth about your life. Although most survivors have been taught to keep the abuse a secret, this silence has been in the best interests of the abusers, not the survivors.

Many survivors want to speak out. Yet each time you consider breaking the taboo of secrecy, you are bound to feel fear and confusion. This is because you are fighting against a system that wants to keep you powerless and silent.

How You Were Silenced

As a child, you might not have told anyone about the abuse. You may have felt ashamed or thought it was your fault. You may have been afraid you'd get punished or that people would think you were bad.

Your abuser may have said, "I'll kill you if you tell," or "You'll be put in jail." If you did get up the nerve to talk, telling may have led to further abuse.

In an ideal world, you would have been believed and comforted. But this probably didn't happen. Instead, it's likely that you were blamed, punished, or called a liar.

If your case went through the court system, you may have been interviewed over and over or forced to face the abuser before you were ready. You may have been blamed for breaking up the family or causing trouble.

Even if these things didn't happen, your story may have been met with silence. No one talked about it. You were told never to bring it up again. You got the message your experience was too horrible for words. And perhaps, that you were too horrible. You learned it wasn't safe to tell the truth.

In other words, you learned shame, secrecy, and silence.

Telling Takes a Leap of Faith

When you first tell someone that you were sexually abused, you may feel both terrified and relieved. Then you may wonder if you've done the right thing. It's scary, and the results are uncertain, but it's important to talk about the abuse. Telling someone has many benefits:

- You face the truth about your abuse.
- You can get help.
- You get more in touch with your feelings.
- You see your experience through the eyes of a person who cares.
- You create deeper, more honest relationships.
- You join a courageous group of survivors who refuse to suffer in silence.
- You help end abuse by breaking the silence in which it thrives.
- You are a model for other survivors.
- You (eventually) feel proud and strong.

To heal from child sexual abuse, you need to tell the truth about your life.

Choosing Someone to Tell

When you first begin talking about your abuse, start with people who are likely to respond well. Begin with the person you trust the most. That might be a counselor, a friend, or your spouse or partner.

A survivors' support group can also be an excellent place to tell your story. As you listen to other survivors, you know you're not alone. And when it's your turn to talk, you experience the understanding and caring of the group.

In time, you need to let the people closest to you know what you're going through. They need to understand why you're upset, why it's hard for you to trust. Your lover needs to know why you're distant or why you don't want sex.

If you're thinking of telling someone, ask yourself:

- Does this person love and respect me?
- Have we been able to talk about personal things before?
- Does this person care about how I feel?
- Do I trust this person? Do I feel safe with this person?

If you can say yes to these questions, you're choosing someone who's likely to support you.

Pick a time when neither of you has to rush off to do something else. And if you want your friend not to tell anyone else, be sure to say so.

At the end of this book, on page 105, the section "For Supporters of Survivors" can help people understand how to respond to you in a helpful way. You might want to ask your friend to read it before you share your story.

When you tell someone and they listen
with respect and caring, your life changes
dramatically.

Confronting Abusers and Other Difficult People

Facing an abuser or telling someone who's likely to get upset or angry is not at all the same as talking to a friend. When you're thinking about a confrontation, you need to prepare in a very different way.

There are many reasons you may want to confront the abuser or talk to people in your family about the abuse. You might want information to help piece together memories. You might want the abuser to feel the impact of what he or she did. Or you might want to find out if an honest relationship is possible with your family.

You might want to protect children who are currently at risk. (*And they are.* We have heard countless stories of survivors who didn't think the abuser would hurt anyone but them. They later found out that their own children, nieces, and nephews had also been abused.)

There is no right or wrong when it comes to confrontations. Some stages of healing are necessary. Confronting abusers and family members is not one of them.

You may have good reasons for not wanting to confront. You may not feel strong enough to face the reaction of your family. You may not have friends or a counselor who can support you. You may have reason to believe you'd be in danger.

Take the time to decide what's right for you.

If you do choose to confront, prepare well:

- **Wait until you're ready.** Work through some of your own feelings before you talk to people who may not be sympathetic.

- **Take your time.** The only exception to this is when children are at risk.

- **Practice.** With friends or a counselor, practice saying the things you want to say. Plan your responses to a wide variety of reactions.

- **Develop realistic expectations.** Honestly assess your expectations. Decide which are realistic, which are unlikely, and which are fantasy.

- **Stay centered.** It's easy to feel like a child when you deal with family members or abusers. Keep a record of contacts with your family or a journal during visits. Carry things that remind you of your current life.

- **Consider bringing along a supportive person**. A friend or counselor may help you feel safer.

- **Put your own needs first.** Don't try to meet family expectations or take care of the abuser's feelings.

Reactions to Telling

It's an honor to listen to the truth of someone's life. When you share difficult truths with someone, they should respect that telling. But that doesn't always happen. Some people are threatened by child sexual abuse. Your story may remind them of things they're not ready to deal with. As a result, people may withdraw or get angry. Some people won't believe you. Others will insist you "get over it." You may even lose some friends or family members who can't deal with your honesty.

Hostile or negative reactions are painful, of course. But other relationships will grow deeper.

To heal from sexual abuse, you need relationships in which you can be your whole self—with your history and your pain. The only way to create those relationships is to share honestly about yourself.

It's an honor to listen to the truth
of someone's life.

Understanding
That It Wasn't
Your Fault

"I know I was only five years old, but I was an extremely intelligent five-year-old. I should have been able to figure out a way to escape."

Most children blame themselves for being sexually abused. Many adult survivors continue to blame themselves. But sexual abuse is *never* the fault of the child.

There are many reasons you may blame yourself for the abuse. The abuser may have told you it was your fault. Your friend's father said, "You're such a sexy little girl, I can't keep my hands off you." Your brother confused you by asking, "You really want to be close to me, don't you?"

You may have been punished if you told. Or called a liar. Your religion may have told you that you were a sinner and that you'd go to hell for the things your coach was making you do. One survivor said:

"I felt like I was really evil. It's like those child-devil movies. Inside this innocent little child is this evil seed. I used to think I made people feel bad and made bad things happen."

As a child, it was too scary to believe that the adults around you were out of control. If you blamed yourself, there was a chance you could fix things by being good. In a strange way, blaming yourself gave you hope.

Survivors blame themselves because they took money, gifts, or special favors. But if you were able to get some small thing back, give yourself credit. One woman was given a bicycle by her abuser. She was able to ride the bicycle into the woods and feel safe. She blamed herself for taking it. Instead she should be praised for finding a way to escape.

Sexual abuse is *never* the fault of the child.

But I Wanted to Be Close

You may feel ashamed because you wanted to be close to the abuser. You needed attention and affection. You weren't getting it anywhere else. So you didn't fight off the sexual advances. Survivors say, "But I'm the one who asked for the back rub," or "I climbed into his bed."

But you were not wrong. Every child needs attention and affection. It's a question of survival. You were meeting an essential need.

Every child needs attention and affection.

But It Felt Good

Some children only feel pain and anguish while they're being abused. But others experience pleasure in their bodies. If the abuse felt good or if you had an orgasm, you may feel particularly ashamed:

> "Some of it felt good, and ugh! It's still hard for me to talk about it. When I think back on times I was close to my mother in a sexual way, where I was getting turned on, there's a lot of shame there. It feels really embarrassing."

One woman was gang-raped as a teenager and had an orgasm. "For a long time I thought it was a cruel joke that God had made my body that way." She desperately needed to know that she wasn't the only survivor who'd had an orgasm while being abused.

It is natural to have sexual feelings when you're touched in a sexual way. The person who is sexually abused and has an orgasm does not want to be abused. Her body simply did what bodies are supposed to do. Her body didn't betray her. The abuser did.

For Saphyre, it's taken a lot of work to overcome the shame:

> "I had to realize I didn't get off because I liked it but because I have a woman's body that is

made to experience passion. My body responded to touch. That is all. And they had no right to mess with that. That anger helped me get over the shame."

But I Was Older

When children are abused, their ability to say no is severely damaged. So even if the abuse continued into adulthood, you are still not to blame. There is no magic age when you suddenly become responsible for your own abuse.

No matter how old you were, no matter what the situation was, there is never an excuse for sexual abuse.

Even if your father is still having sex with you when you are thirty, it is not your fault. You may be an adult in age, but you are still responding like a small, powerless child. If you have been abused your whole life, it is unfair to expect that you'll suddenly be able to say no just because you grow up. If someone with more power is pressuring you into a sexual relationship, you are being abused, no matter how old you are.

Overcoming Shame

The are many ways to overcome shame. One of the most powerful is talking to a trusted person about your abuse:

> "A key sign of healing is that your shame becomes less. Instead of looking at someone's watch while you tell them what happened, you can look at their face. And then eventually you can look in their eyes and tell them, without feeling they can see what a creep you are."

Being in a group with other survivors is also a powerful way to overcome shame. When you hear other survivors tell their stories, you can see the goodness in them. When they listen to you with the same concern and respect, you start to see yourself as a proud survivor who was not to blame. As one survivor put it, "When your counselor says, 'It wasn't your fault,' that's one thing. But when you have eight people saying it to you, it's a lot more powerful."

Speaking out in public can be another way to transform shame into a feeling of power. Many survivors choose to work with abused children, educate the public, or help change outdated laws.

Spending time with children can also give you strong evidence that the abuse wasn't your fault. Children remind you how small and powerless you were when you were young. One mother talked about her daughter:

> "When I saw how little power she had, how small she was when I put her to bed, I got a real

picture of how small and vulnerable *I* had been. I got it in my heart that abuse was not okay. And that I had not been responsible for what had happened to me. I started to forgive myself."

No matter how old you were, no matter what the situation was, there is never an excuse for sexual abuse. If you were abused, it was not your fault.

The Child Within

"I made a real commitment to the child inside myself. I began to feel I wanted her to be a part of me. I wanted to help her feel all right. And I had never felt that before."

Inside all of us, we carry the feelings and the hurts we felt as children. They may be buried, but they are still there. In order to heal, we need to get in touch with these parts of us.

The abuse happened when we were young. It is the child inside who holds the key to our memories and feelings.

When you were a child you had to hide your vulnerability. Being asked to remember it now can feel very threatening. It means remembering your shame and terror. It means remembering a time when you did not have the power to protect yourself.

One survivor believed she made up the abuse as an adult. She couldn't remember being a child at all. Finally, her therapist asked her to bring in childhood pictures. Looking at the pictures, she began to realize that she actually was that child who had been abused.

The child inside you holds the key to your memories and feelings.

Laura remembered herself as a child one Halloween while handing out candy:

"I have always loved children, but for months after I remembered the incest, it was too painful to be around them. I'd see them playing or running down the street, little girls flipping up their skirts and showing white cotton panties. I'd cringe inside, 'They're too vulnerable.'

"I spent Halloween at my friend's house, just a few months after I had my first memories. The doorbell rang. I opened the door to a mother and little girl. The girl was dressed as an angel, in a flowing white dress with gold trim. She had straight blond hair cut in a pageboy. Set on her head was a halo made of aluminum foil and a bent wire coat hanger. I asked her how old she was. 'Five and a half,' she said proudly.

"I couldn't take my eyes off her. She looked exactly like I had when I was her age. It was like looking back twenty-five years. I stared at her until her mother glared at me. I gave the girl a Snickers bar and turned away. I slowly shut the door and sat down in the living room, dazed.

"All I could think was, 'That's how young I was! I was that little when he forced himself on me. How could he have done that?' I felt tears of outrage and grief. I had been innocent! There was nothing I could have done to protect myself. None of it had been my fault. 'I was only a child,' I screamed into the empty living room, the sudden reality of a child of five flooding through me."

Connecting with the Child Within

When you aren't in touch with the younger parts of yourself, you are missing a vital part of who you are. When you hate the child inside you, you hate part of yourself. When you take care of the child inside, you learn to nurture yourself.

When you take care of the child inside, you learn to nurture yourself.

Getting in touch with the child inside means hearing her pain, facing her terror, and comforting her in the night. But it also may bring you rewards you didn't expect.

One woman gave herself kiddie parties on her birthdays. One read children's stories. Another sat down before going to bed and wrote a letter to the child within. "I'd tell her all these nice things. And then I'd get up and read it in the morning."

Get to know the child inside you. You might just learn to play and have a lot more fun.

Grieving

"Sometimes I think I'm going to die from the sadness. Not that anyone ever died from crying for two hours, but it sure feels like it."

As a survivor of child sexual abuse you have a lot to grieve for. You will grieve for the ways you were hurt. You will grieve for not being protected, for the things you missed out on as a child. You will grieve for the time and money it takes to heal, for the relationships and happiness you have lost.

If you covered up your pain by pretending you had a happy childhood, you will have to grieve for the ideal family you didn't really have. You'll have to give up the idea that the abuser had your best interests at heart.

You may have to grieve for the fact that you don't have suitable grandparents for your children, or a family you can depend on.

You must also grieve for the shattered image of a world that is fair and safe for children. You will grieve for your lost innocence and ability to trust.

As a survivor of child sexual abuse you have a lot to grieve for.

Buried Grief

Buried grief poisons you. It limits your ability to feel joy or to be fully alive. An important part of healing is to express the grief you've carried inside.

When you were young, you had to hide your feelings. Now, to move on in your life, you need to go back and relive the experiences you had as a child. You have to feel the grief and anguish, but this time with the support of caring people. You might wonder how going back into the pain can help release you from it. But this is how healing from trauma works.

The way to move beyond grief is to experience your pain fully and honor your feelings. When you face your feelings, and they are met with caring and compassion, they change.

About Grief

You may feel foolish crying over events that happened so long ago. But grief stays stored up until you have a chance to express it.

The way to move beyond grief is to experience
your pain fully and honor your feelings.

Grief has its own timing. You can't say, "This is it.
I'm going to grieve now." You have to make room for
grief as it arises. You need to give yourself the time and
space to let go:

> "I had been in therapy for several months and I
> began to feel safe. There were weeks when I
> entered the building, went up the stairs, and
> checked in, all with a smile on my face. Then
> I'd enter the office, and my therapist would
> close the door. Before she could even get to her
> chair, I'd be crying. Deep within me I held
> those feelings, waiting until I knew there would
> be time and compassion."

However you grieve, allow yourself to release the
feelings you've been holding inside. Grieving can be a
great relief.

Anger

"When I'm angry, it's because I know I'm worth being angry about."

Anger is a natural response to abuse. As a child, you probably weren't allowed to feel or express that anger. So you turned it in on yourself. You may have hated and hurt yourself. You may have stuffed down your anger with food, drugs, or alcohol. Or perhaps you became abusive, using your anger to control and intimidate others.

But anger doesn't have to hurt you or your loved ones. It can be a powerful energy that changes your life.

In order to heal, you must direct your anger at the people who hurt you.

Fear of Anger

Many survivors are afraid of getting angry because their past experiences with anger were frightening or violent.

In your family you may have witnessed anger that was destructive and out of control.

But there is a difference between violence and anger. Anger is a feeling, and feelings, themselves, do not hurt anyone.

When you feel angry, you have choices about how you express that anger. As you welcome your anger and become familiar with it, you can direct it to meet your needs—like an experienced rider controlling a powerful horse.

Anger is a natural response to abuse.

Anger and Love

Anger and love are not incompatible. Most of us have been angry, at one time or another, with everyone we love.

Getting angry at your abuser doesn't have to wipe out the positive parts of your history. You can be furious about the abuse and still hold on to things from your childhood that nourished you.

Often survivors are afraid of getting angry because they're scared they'll lose control. But anger only consumes you when you repress it.

"I'd Like to Kill Him"

Wanting revenge is a sane response to abuse. It's natural to fantasize about revenge. But don't act on your fantasies. If you meet violence with violence, you stoop to the level of your abuser. As one survivor said, "I've learned to respect human life more than he ever did."

There are many ways to positively and safely express your anger. Here are just a few:

- Speak out about sexual abuse.
- Write letters to the abuser. (You don't have to send them.)
- Pound on the bed with a tennis racket.
- Shred sheets of newspaper.
- Break old dishes. (Do it in a safe place.)
- Scream into your pillow.
- Take a self-defense course.
- Organize a survivors' march.
- Fight to change the laws that protect abusers in your state.
- Destroy something the abuser gave you. Enjoy the experience.

The list is endless. Be creative with your anger.

There are many ways to positively and safely

express your anger.

Anger As a Part of Life

As you become more familiar with your anger, it can become a part of your everyday life. When it's not held inside, it stops being a dangerous monster and becomes one of many feelings you might have in a day.

Anger can be so safe that even children aren't scared by it. In Ellen's family, they have a giant stuffed frog they got for two dollars at a garage sale:

> "When one of us gets really angry, we stomp all over it. Even as a very small child, my daughter would explain, 'It's okay to beat up Big Frog because he's not alive. It doesn't really hurt him.' At times when I was crabby she would tell me: 'Go get Big Frog, Mom. You can yell all you want. There's nobody here but me and you, and I don't mind.'"

The Benefits of Anger

Anger motivates us to take action and guides us toward positive change. It can also be the thing that moves us beyond despair:

> "If I was to name one reason I got through it, it would be the anger. I kept saying to myself, 'Are you going to let him win out?' If for no other reason than spite, I forced myself to get better. I was hell-bent on surviving, if only to show him that I was going to outlast him. My anger fueled me to get well. When I would be raging, my therapist would say to me, 'Hold on to that anger. That's your best friend.'"

Women's anger has inspired them to cut ties with abusers, to divorce battering husbands, to quit jobs with abusive bosses, and to break addictions to drugs and alcohol. Focusing anger on the abuser—and away from yourself—clears the way for self-care and positive action in the world.

Anger motivates us to take action and guides us toward positive change.

Forgiveness?

"You don't sit around trying to forgive Hitler. There are a lot of better things to do with a life."

When we talk about the stages of the healing process, the question of forgiveness always comes up. We want to make it clear from the beginning—it is *not* necessary to forgive the abuser in order to heal from child sexual abuse. The only person you have to forgive is *yourself*.

Yet many survivors try desperately to forgive the abuser. They despair that they can't heal without it. But as Ellen says in her workshops, "Why should you? First they steal everything else from you and then they want forgiveness too? Let them get their own. You've given enough."

Eventually you will have to come to some sort of resolution in your feelings about the abuser so you can move on. Whether or not this resolution includes forgiveness is a personal matter.

"Oh Honey, Just Forgive and Forget"

It is insulting to tell a survivor she needs to forgive the person who abused her. Yet you will be given this advice over and over by "well-meaning" people who are uncomfortable with your anger.

When a friend hurts us, she needs to listen to our hurt, admit her error, make amends, and promise to change her behavior in the future. Only then can we forgive her and mend the relationship.

It is the rare abuser who is willing to go this far. And even if they do, it is still up to us to decide when, if, and how we want to forgive.

If you have strong religious beliefs, you may feel it is your sacred duty to forgive. This isn't true. If there is such a thing as divine forgiveness, it's God's job, not yours.

Trying to forgive disrupts the healing process. No one forgives by trying. If forgiveness is to be part of your healing, it will happen only when you've gone through all the other stages of remembering, grief, anger, and moving on. It's a by-product of healing, not the final reward.

It is *not* necessary to forgive the abuser in order to heal from child sexual abuse.

And What If Compassion Sneaks Up on Me?

If it does, let it. Compassion for other people feels good. You may reach a point where you begin to see a family member in a new way:

> "There's a picture in my mind of my mother standing in the hallway with all of us kids. My father was in the bathroom beating my brother. We're all crying, 'Daddy! Daddy!' And my mother's saying, 'Don, don't! Oh, Don, don't!' And she's right there crying with us. She was as much a part of the helplessness as we were. I really believe she did the best she could do. It wasn't very good, but it was the best she could do."

Survivors who naturally come to a place of compassion or forgiveness often feel a new sense of freedom. One woman explained:

> "The intensity in my feelings is gone since I've forgiven him. I don't wake up feeling like if I had his picture, I'd throw daggers at it. I can say, 'Your face no longer scares me. Your name no longer puts me in fear.'"

But They Had a Bad Childhood

Laura remembers her mother coming home from her job as a social worker and telling stories about the people she worked with:

> "She'd take us to Burger Chef, and over the french fries she'd tell us about a sixteen-year-old murderer or a fifteen-year-old rapist. We'd look up from our Cokes and ask, 'But why, Mom? Why would anyone do something like that?' Her answer was always the same. She'd pick up her double hamburger and say, 'They had a bad childhood.'"

It's true that many abusers were abused as children. But that alone is not enough to forgive them for the horrible things they do to children. Many survivors, both women and men, have been sexually abused, and the vast majority of them have not become abusers. Regardless of childhood pain, there is no excuse for abusing children. As one survivor put it:

> "I would never in a million years forgive my father. He had a choice. He made a choice. I've had choices in my life that were just as difficult. Sometimes I've failed. But for the most part I try very hard not to. And I don't think he tried one bit. I think he gave in to his impulses every time."

Forgiving Yourself

The only person you have to forgive is yourself. If you are still blaming yourself or feeling ashamed of the things you've done to cope, you will have to forgive yourself. You will have to stop blaming the child who was vulnerable, the child who felt pleasure, the child who survived the best she could.

The only person you have to forgive is yourself.

You must forgive yourself for not knowing how to protect yourself or your children, or for abusing others. You must forgive yourself for needing the time to heal now. And you must give yourself all the kindness and compassion you can, so you can direct your attention and energy toward your own healing. *This* forgiveness is what's important.

Spirituality

"There was a voice inside of me that just said, 'You'll get there.' And I took hope and courage from that voice. It was my spirituality."

Finding the spiritual part of yourself can be an important part of healing. Yet many survivors have lost their faith. "Pillars of the church" sexually abused them. God didn't protect them. One woman explained:

> "I was in a very conservative religious group for twenty years. I thought Jesus could heal me. When I started having memories of sexual abuse, the first thing I thought was, 'What kind of God have I been believing in?' A little girl had been beaten and raped and no God did anything about it."

Spirituality can help to heal this kind of loss. You feel connected to life around you. You experience this in nature as you watch waves roll in, look out over vast prairies, or walk in the desert. You touch this special place when you hold a new baby, listen to inspiring music, or connect deeply with someone you love. It's the miracle of life.

When you see cocoons turn into butterflies, it's just a little easier to believe that a damaged human being can become whole—even if that human being is you. Spirituality means staying in touch with the part of you that is choosing to heal, that wants to be healthy and fully alive.

When you can see that cocoons turn into butterflies, it's just a little easier to believe that a damaged human being can become whole— even if that human being is you.

The person you want to become is already with you. You just can't always see her. Getting in touch with the stillness inside you can help you see you are more than just a person in pain.

Finding Faith

Survivors often obsess about healing. They think about little else. Some of this is natural and unavoidable. But beyond a certain point, it can hinder you.

Often we obsess about our abuse because we don't believe the healing process is really working. We think we have to try hard every minute or we'll lose ground. This isn't true. We often make our greatest strides when we give ourselves room to absorb the healing work we've already done.

As you relax and trust your ability to heal yourself, you gain confidence that you will make it. You start to believe in yourself.

A Personal Thing

A spiritual connection is a very personal thing. Your spirituality may stem from a religion, from the safety you feel in your support group, or from trusting your instincts. No one can tell you how to do it right.

Yet believing in something more constant than your own shifting emotions can be a great comfort as you heal. Spirituality can be a source of inspiration, courage, and love.

Spirituality can be a source of inspiration, courage, and love.

The Process of Change

"My grandfather was dead and gone and I was alive with the same problems I'd always had. I had to face the fact that if I wanted a different life, I was going to have to do something about it."

When you first start dealing with your abuse, you may be relieved to finally have someone to blame for your problems. There is a reason for your suffering. You were sexually abused.

But eventually, you realize things aren't that simple or fair. It's not enough to know you were abused. You also have to change your life. One survivor explained:

> "I had to go from dealing with the incest an hour a week in therapy to dealing with it in my real life. I *changed* my relationship. I *changed* my job. I *changed* my home. I started getting angry.

I started to cry. I've really changed. I *look* different. I *sound* different. I *changed* my life."

It's not enough to know you were abused. You
also have to change your life.

How to Change

- **Become aware of the behavior you want to change.**
  Is there something you're doing that isn't good for
  you? Are you staying in a bad relationship? Are you
  drinking too much? Are you helping everyone
  except yourself?

- **Look at the reasons you developed that behavior
  to begin with.** When did you first feel or act that
  way? Why?

- **Have compassion for what you've done in the past.**
  Even if you didn't make the best choices, you did
  the best you could at the time. And now you can
  make better choices. Focus on that.

- **Find new ways to meet your needs.** When you
  learn to fulfill your needs in new ways, it will be
  easier to let go of your old behavior.

- **Get support.** The people around you affect your
  ability to change. People who are working to grow
  in their lives will support your efforts to change.

- **Name your fears.** It's scary to change. We usually
  give something up in order to make room for

something new. Looking at why you're scared can lessen the power of your fears.

- **Fear doesn't have to stop you.** Everyone feels scared when they change, even if it's a change for the better. If you're scared, act anyway.

- **Old habits don't change easily.** When you try to change an old habit, it sometimes seems to get worse. Don't give up at this critical point. The "I can't stand it anymore" feeling often means you're close to the change you've been wanting to make.

- **Make several tries.** Making changes is usually a slow trial and error process. Yet each little step forward leads to real change and a better life.

- **Keep trying.** Don't give up. Most of the changes we make in life require repetition. If not smoking *one* cigarette were enough, it wouldn't be so hard to quit smoking.

- **Be gentle with yourself.** Be patient. Forgive yourself when you go back to an old behavior you're trying to change. Don't punish yourself.

- **Give yourself credit.** Take time to feel proud of yourself when you have a success. Don't just run to the next mountain.

- **Celebrate.** Treat yourself well when you have a victory.

Resolution and Moving On

"I feel like I'm home free. I still have a lot of work to do, but I know it can be done. I know what the tools are and I know how to use them. When I talk about the incest now, a lot of it is about the healing and the success and the joy."

—Saphyre

Jean Williams is an incest survivor and the child of alcoholic parents. After many years of healing, she had an experience that dramatically changed her point of view:

> "I went to Mexico for a few months and I really learned a lot by living in another culture. When I came back my mail was full of fliers about self-improvement programs. And I thought, 'My God! I don't want to improve myself anymore. I'm good enough the way I am!'"

Moving on can't be forced or rushed. Yet from the moment you begin to deal with the abuse, people will urge you to hurry up and "put it in the past." There will be times you want to "move on" as well—simply because healing is so painful. But moving on to escape the pain or to please others is an escape.

Real moving on is the natural result of fully living through each step of the healing process.

Feeling More Stable

Resolution comes when your feelings and point of view become steadier. The emotional roller coaster evens out. You begin to see your life as more than just a reaction to abuse:

> "You can look at my life and say there've been some real tragedies, and there have been. But there've also been some exquisitely beautiful times. To me, those far outweigh the others."

As you put the abuse you suffered in perspective, it becomes one part of your history, not your whole life.

Resolving Relationships

Part of moving on is coming to terms with the people who abused you, didn't protect you, or don't support you now. You get a clear idea of how you feel about each of them. You decide what, if any, relationship you want with them in the future.

Survivors often waste precious energy hoping to get people in their lives to change, apologize, or take responsibility. For the most part, these wishes are fantasies.

When you come to a place of resolution with your family or the abuser, the effect is often dramatic. When you stop hoping for the impossible, you open the doors for real help and support to come in.

Letting Go of the Damage

There may be times in the healing process when you lose touch with the fact that you're working so hard *in order to move on to something else in life*. Being a survivor is painful, but it can also bring you a sense of identity and pride that can be hard to give up:

> "A lot of people get stuck in the rage and hatred and fear. But I realized I didn't have to hang on to it. I stopped sitting there picking open wounds, saying, 'If only I pick deep enough, I can see some real blood and gore.' I wanted to feel safe in the world.
>
> "There was a point where I simply stopped carrying the bags. Every now and then the porter brings it to me and says, 'Here's your baggage, ma'am.' And I open it up and go through it again. And then I say, 'I've seen enough of you for now. I want to go on with my

life again.' And life feels much better. It's a
tremendous relief to stop suffering all the time."

Letting Go of Crisis

It's easy to get used to intensity and drama, but being in
constant crisis keeps you from moving on. It's a major
milestone when you stop generating one crisis after
another. Yet you're likely to feel empty and uncertain
when there's no emergency to cope with. Wait it out. The
rewards are worth it.

When you learn to balance life's challenges with
quiet, peaceful times, you make room to enjoy some of
the smaller, daily pleasures. Cooking dinner, taking walks,
growing flowers, and listening to music can be deeply satisfying.

Part of healing is doing the things you've always
wanted to do. You don't have to wait until you're
"completely healed" to begin enjoying your
present life.

Healing is not about endless struggle. Part of healing is doing the things you've always wanted to do. You
don't have to wait until you're "completely healed" to
begin enjoying your present life.

And it's only when you're not in crisis that you can work toward some of your dreams.

Becoming Whole

As you heal, you see yourself more realistically. You accept that you are a person with strengths and weaknesses. You make the changes you can in your life and let go of things that aren't in your power to change.

You learn that every part of you is valuable. And you realize that all of your thoughts and feelings are important, even when they're painful or difficult:

> "I thought when you were healed, everything felt good, but it isn't true. I wanted to select certain things—humor, warmth, love, fun. I didn't want to feel scared or angry or any 'negative feelings.' But they're all part of being human."

Every part of you is valuable and important.

There Is No End of the Line

There is no finish line to healing. You can't erase your history. The abuse affected you deeply. That will never change. But you can come to a place of peace, gradually accepting that the healing process will continue throughout your life:

> "Finally, I had to realize it was part of me. It's not something I can get rid of. The way I work with it will change, but it will always be there. If I'm going to love myself totally, then I have to love all of me, and this is part of who I am."

Most survivors make the decision to heal from a place of pain, shame, and terror. At the beginning, the work feels like a burden. But eventually, you realize that healing has brought you more than just the lessening of pain. You start to see the healing process as the beginning of a lifetime of growth. As one survivor put it, "I have no intention of stopping. I fully intend to grow until I die."

At the beginning, the work feels like a burden. But eventually, you see the healing process as the beginning of a lifetime of growth.

Part Two

Courageous Women

After You Tell: Janel's Story

Janel Robinson is nineteen years old and of Native American, Peruvian, and Irish heritage.* She lives with her mother, stepfather, and fourteen-year-old brother, works part-time selling newspaper ads, and is completing her A.S. degree at her local community college. Janel studies computer science and would someday like to have a career helping other survivors of sexual abuse.

I was molested by two of my grandfathers. The first molestation started when I was two and went on until I was six. The only reason anybody found out was that I

---

* Janel chose to use a pseudonym.

kept having bladder infections. The doctor found bruises in my vulva. That's how everything came out.

I remember being questioned with anatomical dolls, but I didn't really know what was going on. My mom stuck me into counseling for a little while, but I didn't like it. There was this big dark hallway we had to go through and it scared me, so after a while we stopped going.

My family handled the first molestation fairly well. My grandmother was shocked, but she helped with the prosecution. She said, "This is what we have to do. This is what's right." The whole family helped out. My grandfather was convicted and sent to jail.

When I was nine or ten, my cousin told me my other grandfather had been molesting her for years. At first, I didn't believe her. It was too shocking. I'd blocked out the earlier molestation. But after she told me, I stopped and said, "Wait a minute! That happened to me before!"

My cousin went to my grandfather and said, "Tell her it's true." He said, "Okay. We're going to play a little game. Take off all your clothes." I just stood there in shock.

My grandfathers knew each other and they talked about the molestation. I guess he figured since it had happened to me already, it was okay to do it again.

He molested us for the next year. I kept telling my cousin, "We need to say something." Finally we made a plan to tell our parents the same weekend. I went home and told and she went home and didn't. Our grandfather was convicted and went to jail. And that whole side of the family resented me.

The hardest thing for me was that my parents wanted to stay on good terms with my grandfather and that side of the family. They pushed me to go over there for holidays and then I'd get shunned. It was awful.

My relatives hated me because I had put him in jail. One even implied I was the one who had initiated the molestation. He told me, "From now on you better mind your parents and be a good little girl."

That was the last time I went over there. I started staying home by myself on holidays. That's what started the healing process for me—taking a stand and saying, "I'm not going to put myself through that."

Everyone protected my grandfather. The family kept sweeping it under the rug. Even my cousin protected him. When he got out of jail, she and my brother continued to go to his house. He started molesting both of them again. And he was sent back to jail.

After he was convicted the second time, my parents finally came to the conclusion, "This is not right." They only have minimal contact with my grandfather now.

How the Abuse Affected Me

I started acting out some time after the second molestation. I didn't know why. I didn't connect it to the molestation. I just thought I was a bad person who was going in the wrong direction.

I did drugs, marijuana and LSD. I carved on myself. I was promiscuous. I didn't get along with anybody. I hated myself.

I remember being in the fifth grade and thinking of suicide.

By my freshman year in high school, I was doing a lot of cocaine. I did it to feel better about myself. I also thought I was fat and wanted to lose weight. But I was really skinny. That was another reason. When you do cocaine, you feel great. You're on top of the world. But when you come down, you feel awful, like you're the lowest person in the world.

When I was thirteen and coming down from cocaine, I tried to kill myself. My mother and I had been arguing. I wanted to go out and she didn't want to let me. I was wearing a miniskirt and she said I looked like a slut. Something clicked in my brain. I said to myself, "Even my mom thinks I'm a slut. Everyone thinks I'm a slut because I was abused. So it's all my fault." Boom. I ran into the bathroom and slit my wrists. I didn't really realize what I was doing till I started bleeding all over the place. I didn't feel anything.

My mom didn't know what to do with me. She put me in bed and watched me all night long. Two days later, she took me to the emergency room and I was hospitalized.

Starting to Heal

Being in the hospital was comforting. I'd hit such a bottom, I didn't resist it.

It was a women's hospital. There were adults and teenagers there. The majority of women had been sexually abused. Sharing with them was really helpful I was able to say, "Here's my story. This is what happened to me." That was a real turning point for me. I learned that I was not the only one. I started realizing I had a lot of problems and that they were related to the molestation.

It was almost like a type of school. All I did there was learn. I learned a lot about me. It was wonderful. I was still feeling confused and introverted and not so hot about myself, but at least I had some insight to work with.

After a month, my insurance ran out. My psychiatrist went on vacation and the person who took his place said, "You're out of here." My psychiatrist came back and said, "Where is she?" I wasn't supposed to be released, but they released me anyhow.

When I went home, I was really depressed: I wasn't eating or sleeping. I wasn't functioning. My mom said, "I don't know how to deal with this," and she put me in a group home. She said, "They can deal with you."

Initially we were going to do a six-week trial period—a kind of assessment. I thought, "Six weeks, no problem. That's half my summer vacation—I can deal with that." Six weeks passed and I said, "Okay, Mom. I'm ready to come home." And she said, "No, you're not. We really aren't ready to deal with you." So I said, "Screw you," and stayed in the group home.

Three or four times we made a date for me to come home, and that day would roll around and pass. She kept saying I wasn't ready, that she didn't think she was ready. Looking back, I realize she didn't feel capable of dealing with me. She didn't think she could handle it if I had a really bad day and felt suicidal. I don't really blame her. Now. But at the time, I really resented it. It was really disappointing. I had to separate myself from my mom and say, "I'm my own person. I don't need to be so attached to you."

I was in a group home for a year. There were meetings twice a week. We saw psychologists and counselors and social workers. It was very structured and I think that was helpful. Looking back, I'm extremely thankful I was there.

After a year, I finally went home. At first my parents tried to structure everything—they overstructured it for the first couple of months. We argued a lot. My mom threatened to send me back to the group home. But after that, we laid out everything straight and said, "Here's your space. This is ours." We worked it out. I'm still living with them and it's great.

Confronting My Grandfathers

While I was in the hospital, I decided I wanted to confront my first grandfather. He molested me from the time I was two until I was six, yet I only remembered three incidents. Obviously, I'd repressed a lot because I lived with him for quite a while, and this was a regular thing that went on, probably every day. But I couldn't remember it, and that really scared me.

I found out he had cancer. I decided to confront him before he died. I wanted some closure. I wanted to find out what happened to me rather than spending lots of money on a hypnotist. So we had a confrontation. I talked to him for an hour. It was really scary. He told me just about everything that he had done to me.* He said, "I didn't do anything bad to you. You liked it. You kept coming back. I just gave you what you wanted." I said, "A two-year-old doesn't know what's right and wrong." He couldn't really say anything to that. When he died a couple of years ago, I was really glad I'd talked to him.

We sued my second grandfather. It wasn't my idea, but I felt good about it. My mother called me while I was in the hospital and said, "Guess what? We're suing your grandfather." She said, "If you can't get them to stay in jail long enough, the best way you can get them is where it really hurts—in their pocketbook." I knew the hospital was really expensive. I thought, "If this is going to put my parents in a financial bind, maybe this is what we should do."

It was a really long process. He made me go through a deposition. It lasted two or three hours. He had three different lawyers there. They didn't even want to let my mom in with me. It was really scary. I was only thirteen.

The deposition was almost like a court trial, the kind you see on TV. It was awful. They asked everything. I've blocked out a lot of it, but I remember them asking me if I was a virgin. One of the lawyers began to explain to me the process of losing your virginity and what happens with the breaking of the hymen. I was shocked. I thought, "How could this pertain to my grandfather molesting me?" I just looked at him and said, "That's

---

* Janel's experience with her grandfather is unusual. Most perpetrators deny the abuse and aren't reliable sources for finding out what happened to you.

none of your damn business." He asked me again, and the lawyers got into an argument.

They asked me every personal question in the book: what boyfriends I had, how my other grandfather molested me. They asked me more questions about my personal life than they did about the molestation. They tried to minimize the molestation, saying, "Isn't it true he only did this to you?" They made me feel really bad. When I walked out of there, I felt really small, like I was the bad person.

It's awful how the justice system makes victims feel that way. I think people being accused of the crime should go through that—not the victim. If the victim says, "This happened to me," why should they be questioned and bugged about it? It's just a tactic lawyers use to scare the victim. I don't think they should be allowed to do it.

I Think the System Is Really Screwy

The system—the criminal justice system, the social workers, the police—handle these things terribly. A lot of kids are abused, and the system says, "Okay, we're going to take you out of your home." Why do they have to take the kids out of the home? Why can't they put the abuser somewhere else? Why do they have to disrupt the child's life? While I was in the group home there were two or three girls I knew personally who had been in ten foster homes, two or three group homes, different shelters, juvenile hall, out on the street, thrown here, there, and everywhere. Personally, I don't think it's good for kids to be shuffled around like that.

When I was in the group home I met this girl who was my age. We had the same status; we'd gone through a lot of the same stuff. Both of us had been abused. Neither of us had ever broken any laws. By the time she left the group home, she had a police record. She ended up killing herself.

That was really hard on me. She was a good friend. We were in exactly the same boat. She went in one direction and I went in the other. She came to the group home to get therapy and become more stable. I believe the system made her worse. She fell through the cracks. A lot of kids do.

Where I Am Today

Once I figured out that a lot of my problems stemmed from the abuse, I knew I needed to deal with them. I had a lot of determination. I wasn't going to let anybody or anything stop me.

I'm still healing. I'm not in as intense therapy as I was, but it still affects me. I still have trouble trusting people and trusting my own judgment.

For a while I had trouble being sexual. I'd look at my boyfriend's face and all of a sudden it would be my grandfather. It was awful. My boyfriend and I worked through that. It took quite a while, but he has a lot of patience. He listened. He went to counseling with me.

We read books together. Anytime I'd have a memory or flashback, he'd be there. He'd listen and comfort me. Now my sex life is great.

I'm proud of coming as far as I have. I can say to myself, "Hey I survived that, and I'm still here."

Going through what I've gone through has made me a stronger person. I've converted the pain into tools and knowledge that I can apply to problems that come up now. I'm proud of that.

If I was talking to another teenager in my situation, I'd say, "Hang in there. It's tough, but it gets better. It may not seem like it, but it does. It's a process you have to go through."

I Told My Son: Eva's Story

Eva Smith is an African-American in her early thirties who lives in California.* She is a therapist and an artist. She lives with her two teenage children. "I share this information as a gift of healing for other women. I am truly living my life now, after just surviving for so many years."

Between the ages of three and eight, I was molested by my great uncle. From nine to fifteen, my stepfather molested me. I grew up just trying to live from day to day and survive. I used to pray my stepfather would get struck by lightning. I wasn't above making a pact with the devil

---

* Eva Smith chose to use a pseudonym.

to get rid of him. *Anything*. And anything happened. I got pregnant.

I had always been a fat child. When I was thirteen, I weighed 188 pounds. And then I lost weight. So when I got pregnant, everybody just thought I was getting fat again. I'll never forget—I was going into my junior year in high school and my mother and I went shopping for clothes. She came into the dressing room, looked at me, and said, "You look different." And I said, "I'm just getting fat again." And she said, "I'm taking you to the doctor." That was in September, and considering that my son was born in November, I must have been at least seven months pregnant, but all this was brand new to me.

When the doctor told my mother I was pregnant, she asked me who the father was, and I told her. She confronted my stepfather and he claimed that he knew nothing about it. Within a week, we left him and went down South.

When I first realized I was pregnant, I attempted suicide. It was a hard time for me. *I* knew I needed therapy. I wish somebody else realized it at the time!

My mother told me I didn't have to keep the child. She said I could put it up for adoption or that she would raise it as her own. I chose to keep that child because it was the first thing that was ever mine.

I created a cover story about who the father was. I said he was some boy I'd been going with. I had to deal with a lot of put-downs from people, you know, cause I was fifteen and having this baby.

Because of all the things that happened to me, there was this question that used to haunt me, you know, "Why me?" Those were the years I call my trauma years.

And I went from my trauma years into being a battered wife.

He Had the License

I got married at seventeen. I was already pregnant with my daughter. We were already into it before we ever got married. We used to argue once a week when we were going together, but not real physical stuff. But after we were married, he had the license. You know, they pronounce you man and *wife*, not man and *woman*. To my way of thinking it gives men a free ticket to do whatever they want. So the battering started and increased till I couldn't take it.

I was making $1.79 an hour. I was paying all the bills. I was buying all the food, the clothes, even renting him a television. I got off work at 4:30. I was supposed to catch the bus at 4:35, hit downtown at 5:00, change buses, and walk in the door at 5:20. If I walked in the door at 5:30, I got my ass kicked.

So in essence, he held my children hostage. He did lots of sadistic things to me. My nerves were so bad, I was going through temporary blindness. I was on a large dose of Librium.

I was twenty then, and I tried to kill myself. I had gotten my prescription filled. I came home and took half the bottle. He found the bottle and woke me up 'cause I was going off to la-la land. And he got me up and went and got my son, who was four at the time. He sprayed Raid in his hair, then he took a lighter and held it over his head and said, "If you don't wake up, I'm gonna light his hair." I mean I was going through it. We didn't have a phone or anything. There's that isolation thing.

I decided to kill him. I knew we couldn't live together without one of us killing the other. So I was going to kill him. I planned that Friday when I got paid, I'd pay the rent, the water bill, buy a gun, go home, walk in the door, scream, and kill him. Even now, I can say with conviction I was going to kill him.

And this woman who was like my second mother said, "You don't want that on your head for the rest of your life." So I turned him over to the military 'cause he'd gone AWOL. They took him to jail. I took the children to safety and moved out in four days. I started divorce proceedings immediately.

When I got rid of my husband, all that weird stuff went away. The blindness and the shaking went away. I didn't have to take Librium.

So by the time I was twenty-one, I had been married, divorced, and had two children. When I moved to California, I had seven suitcases, two kids, and one hundred dollars. And Lord, I've come a long way from there.

I Have Told My Son

My son will be eighteen this fall, and when he was thirteen, I told him who his father was. He had been asking questions on a regular basis. When he was younger, I told him my cover story—that his father was a teenager I had sex with. That was okay then, but as he got older, when he'd ask questions about his father, there'd be a hush in the room or people would change the subject. So he got the feeling there was this secret. A number of people were in on this secret, and he wasn't one of them. There's no father on his birth certificate, so there was always this air of mystery. And at thirteen he just asked me in a more straightforward way than he ever had before, so I told him.

Ahmal—the man I was involved with at the time, who was a father figure for my children—and I got together and discussed it thoroughly. And then the three of us went into the bedroom. My son was trying to be grown up, wanting to have a cigarette. Everybody was cool, you know. I think it's important to say how I told it to him because I didn't make it a real heavy-duty kind of thing.

I'm a storyteller, and I just told it like you'd tell any kind of story to a child. I had parts in it that made him laugh. I told it in a way that wasn't condemning my stepfather, because no matter how much pain he brought into my life, this man was my son's biological father, and whatever I told him was going to mold a certain part of him for the rest of his life. So it was important to me not to make my stepfather an ogre, to tell my son about it in such a way that he would not be as devastated as I was by it. Your children are more important than anything that may hurt you or the hate that you feel.

And so I dredged up every good memory about my stepfather that I could find. I worked at making him very human. I talked about his shortcomings and the good things about him. I talked about his smile, 'cause he had a wonderful smile. I didn't go into the sexual abuse real heavy because that was not the important thing at that point. I talked about what he did to me and how young I was. I put in a little drama, 'cause there was plenty of that, but I didn't make it a great big thing. And I talked about what it was like being pregnant with him. How I felt. I was fifteen. How that felt.

My son's first reaction was, "Wow, all of that happened to me!" And Ahmal said, "Hey, blood, check this out. None of that happened to you. It happened to your mother." And so my son had to deal with that. He had to weigh how this affected who he was as a person. It was a very difficult time for him. And it was a very, very hard time for me because he was trying to punish me for who his father was.

Slowly it has healed for my son. Now it's just a fact of being. I don't think he resents me for it. If anything, maybe he loves me a little more. He was a spirit that had to come here and that was the way he came.

It Only Happened Once: Vicki's Story

Vicki is a forty-year-old Jewish lesbian mother who lives with her partner and their two children.* Her story is important because it speaks to all the survivors who believe their abuse doesn't count because it only happened once. But as Vicki's story shows, all abuse is harmful.

There was always a creepy feeling in my house of my father being really inappropriate. He'd be too close. He was always kissing me too long. It got worse when I was a teenager. My girlfriends felt weird around him and he was really hostile to my boyfriends.

My father only molested me once, when I was

---

* Vicki chose to use a pseudonym.

twelve years old. I was asleep in bed. He came into my room and lay down next to me. He put his hand down my pajamas and started playing with my vagina. It woke me up. I turned away from him. I pretended I was turning over in my sleep. He must have gotten frightened that I would wake up, and he left. I remember watching his shadow outside the door. He never did it again.

Before he molested me, I felt very free in my body. I felt wonderful. I was coming into puberty. I was outgoing and friendly. I had boyfriends. Everything was waking up. And my first intimate sexual experience was with my father. He was the first man to ever touch my genitals.

It was very upsetting and confusing to me. I loved my father. We had a really strong relationship. After he molested me, I went into a deep depression. I shut out the outside world. This veil just came down, and that was it. It took me until I was twenty-two to even realize that something was wrong.

I never forgot what happened. It just went underground. I didn't think about it a lot, but it's had long-lasting effects. I've had a difficult time getting close to my lovers. I need a lot of control in my relationships.

I never compared what happened to me to what other people went through because I really knew the hell inside myself. You don't have to have it happen over and over to know, "This is really terrible." It doesn't take much to feel the devastation of a parent crossing those boundaries.

If I was talking to someone who said, "Oh, well, he just fondled me a little bit. It's not such a big deal," I'd ask, "When you connect with another human being in a deep way, how does it make you feel? Does it make you feel scared? Like closing down? Or like really being close to that person?" Really check it out with yourself. Then think about whether you were affected.

It counts if it keeps you from being close to another person. It counts if you're missing a part of yourself. Even if it only happened once, it counts.

Learning to Survive: Soledad's Story

Soledad is a twenty-eight-year-old Chicana who was severely abused by her father throughout her childhood.* Today she is a high school counselor in Sonoma County, California.

Soledad writes, "In this interview, I have spoken more of my biological parents (due to my feelings of betrayal and violation) than of my Tias and Tio, who were very much my parents, in the true sense of the word. Without them, I am con-

---

* Soledad chose to use a pseudonym.

vinced I would not have survived. I am certain my life would have been beaten or suffocated out of me. To them I owe my life. And because of them, I will struggle to keep it.

"I once read that we can give two things to children—one is a sense of roots and the other is a sense of wings. I now know my roots, my history. Now I am ready to fly toward the sun."

Being Latina is real precious to me. However, part of the culture I hate is the silence. As beautiful as our language is, we don't have words for this. Our history is passed orally, yet there's such silence in Latino families about this.

There was no talk about sex in the house ever. It was all out on the streets. And how can you go to a woman you haven't been able to talk to about your damn period and tell her that her husband is raping you?

I think this kind of silence might be common, but it's especially true because my people feel so powerless in this culture, fearing authorities outside the family. We had to stick together and protect each other from the system, and the white people who control it. What other options did we have? We just had to keep it in. Admitting any problem would reflect badly on our whole culture.

And that's why it's hard for me to talk about it. I don't want anyone to use this against people of color, because there are so many negative stereotypes of Latinos already. And I don't want to promote more distrust of men of color. But this is how it happened for me and I need to break the silence.

My Father Was Like a Volcanic Eruption

I was raised in an extended family in Los Angeles in a hard-core ghetto. I'm the oldest of three kids. My dad worked on and off in factories. My mom worked in sweatshops. We not only lived in poverty, we *were* poverty.

I was beaten at least every other day for years. I hated that my parents beat us, but everybody around us got whipped, so that was just the way it was. At least when my mother beat us, we still had a feeling she loved us. It hurt less.

My father was like a volcanic eruption. You wouldn't know when it was going to happen, but when it did, there was no stopping it. He wore these steel-toed shoes for work, and he'd kick us everywhere, including the head. You could get arrested for kicking a dog like that.

My father not only molested me, he molested all my cousins and all the girls in the neighborhood. The ones that I know, there are at least twenty-four. People trusted him with their kids. He was a great social manipulator. He knew how kids thought. It's amazing how one person can mess with so many kids.

From what I can tell, the sexual abuse started right when I was brought home from the hospital. In the beginning there was a lot of fondling. He could be what you would call "gentle," but I would interpret that as being sneaky, because I knew he could kill me. If you know that this man can kill you so easily, you're not going to say anything. And so I would just be frozen, with the feeling, "Soon it will be over." But it got worse and worse.

The peak of it all was at about eight. That's when he first raped me. It was pretty regular after that, at least three times a week. It happened in a lot of different places. We lived in really small quarters with no privacy. So he'd tell me we had to go out for milk, or that we needed to go for a ride in the car. He loved to take all the girls out for a ride. Most of this stuff happened in the car, a lot of it in the dark, so this left a blank for me because a lot of it I didn't see.

A lot of the raping happened from behind. When he abused me, he would talk to me in Spanish, threatening to cut my throat or cut my tongue out. So now, telling you my story in English is easier. I would probably be sobbing by now if I was describing what he had done in Spanish.

When I was thirteen the sexual abuse stopped. I had gotten more streetwise than ever, and he started to be fearful of me. He knew I was ready to die, and that I would fight him to our graves if I had to.

I Lived on the Streets

I was very self-destructive. I started taking drugs at nine. I started hustling. I did drugs and wouldn't even know what the hell I was taking. I didn't care.

Fighting was an everyday thing on the streets. As we got bigger, the toys got more dangerous. I carried knives. I got into fights with people who carried knives. And some with guns. You never knew if you'd come out alive.

Between what was happening at home and having to fight on the streets, I always thought the only freedom would be to go to prison. Then I would be free.

I dealt with my life hour by hour. For a long time, I never did want to live. I'd be five and I'd think, "Maybe I won't live until I'm ten," and I would hope that would be true. Or I'd get to be ten, and I'd think, "Okay, fifteen, max. That's as long as I'm going to live."

What other choices did I have? I grew up poor. Life was just the way it was. I never knew there was a way out.

There Was More to Life Than What I Knew

I was always in and out of school. I was illiterate. But a teacher took an interest in me when I was sixteen. She cared about me and thought I had a good mind. She was scared of me but wanted to find out why I was the way I was. She started talking to me and spending time with me. It mattered to her that I didn't destroy myself. And that made all the difference. There wasn't anyone before who had ever spent that kind of time with me.

Learning to read helped me see that there was more to life than what I knew. That was the beginning of my healing. It was the first time I thought that maybe I could survive without hustling. Maybe I could learn something from some book and get some power from it. Get some options.

I was lucky. I got into an Upward Bound program. She helped me get into college. It was a real culture shock. I hadn't ever been around that many white people. I still couldn't read enough to understand the menus in the cafeteria. But I stuck it out.

I Was Barely Keeping Myself Alive

Even though I succeeded in going to school and getting a job, I knew things weren't right inside. For a long time all I did was come home and lay on my bed. Sometimes I'd turn the TV on. My dinner would be a Coke. Maybe I'd decide to have a real dinner, and I'd have a pint of ice cream. That was my life. I'd never open the drapes, answer the phone, or open the door. I was barely keeping myself alive.

About a year and a half ago, my cousin called me up and said, "Did you know that your dad molested my sisters?"

I said, "I never really thought about him that way. But it doesn't surprise me."

I went over to visit her and we stayed up the whole

night and the whole day to talk about it. It was painful, but I felt vindicated. I knew I wasn't crazy. There were reasons I was destroying myself. I finally knew why I hated him so much. I had always thought people were born hating their fathers.

From then on, I couldn't stop thinking about it. I was obsessed. And I started to understand all these things. I started to wake up feeling powerful. I'd always had to carry a knife or be hustling to feel powerful before. All of a sudden I had a belief in myself.

I Never Had Plants Before

I feel lighter, like a real burden has come off me. If I had run away from the pain, I think I would still be destroying myself in some way.

It's a small thing, but I never had plants before. It's my way of trying to keep something other than me alive. It gives me a lot of pleasure. I grew up where there weren't too many flowers, right in the middle of the damn city.

I got my first plant about six months ago. Now I have all sorts of flowers on my porch. I have big bushes with purple flowers. I have big round pots with different flowers in them. I wanted color around me. It's real Latina, all these colors. It reminds me a lot of my aunts.

It's a reason to live, really. I was scared about it at first. But now I know I can nurture them and keep them healthy. After I've been so rough in my life, I can still take care of something so delicate.

I Loved My Father:
Randi's Story

Randi Taylor is thirty years old.* She is single, lives alone, and works as a restaurant manager in Seattle. She was raised in an upper-middle-class white family of European descent. Randi has two sisters and two brothers.

Randi was always Daddy's girl. She idolized her father. The molestation occurred when Randi was twelve to fourteen, just as she was going through puberty. It always was hidden in games and laughing.

---

* Randi Taylor wanted to use her own name but couldn't for legal reasons.

I never saw anyone like me in the incest books. I never saw anyone who had a good relationship with her father. All the perpetrators looked like angry, ugly, mean people, and yet my father appeared to be a loving, charming, wonderful man. I loved and adored him. He treasured me.

My father and I would do a lot of fun things together. I'd pour a glass of water on his head, and he'd pour a glass of water on mine. We'd be tickling and wrestling and chasing each other around the house. A lot of times when he was tickling me, he'd reach his hand around and cup my breast. I'd always scream at him not to do that, but my screams would get mixed up with all the laughter and hilarity and screaming that was already going on. I'd tell him to stop and he'd say, "Oh gee, did I slip? I didn't mean to." He made a mockery of it.

Whenever we rode in the car, I'd sit in the middle of the front seat. When we went around a sharp turn, my father would elbow my boobs. He'd do it on purpose, always with an exaggerated gesture. My sisters and I had a name for it. We said my father was "boobing" me.

Then there was a routine we went through every morning. I'd get up to brush my teeth. When I came back to my room I'd have to search in my closet or under my bed because my father would be hiding there, waiting for me to undress. I knew he wanted to see me naked. I'd have to chase him out. I had to protect myself from this Peeping Tom who was my father. But it was made into a game. It was just a normal part of the Taylor family morning routine.

At one point my father took up a sudden interest in photography, but he only wanted to photograph his daughters. He made me wear a thin T-shirt and he shined a light from behind my boobs. He wanted a picture of my boobs showing through a filmy T-shirt.

While he was doing the photos, his hands would get shaky. His breath would be louder than normal. He would be excited. It was very scary for me to see him that way. Here was this man I adored. He was out of control and I never knew how far he would go.

One time, my mother was going to be away all day. I was home sick from school. And in the middle of the day, my father came home from work. I was very frightened. I said, "What are you doing here?" He was joking and smiling and happy. "Oh, I thought I'd come home to see you. I knew you were here by yourself not feeling good."

He'd brought home some felt-tipped pens, and the game he had in mind was to decorate my breasts. He made me pull up my nightgown and he drew on my body. He made my two breasts into eyes, and then he drew a nose and mouth beneath it. His hands were shaking and his breath was really hot while he was doing that. And all the time, he was joking and teasing. It was horrible for me. Yet it was the one experience that allowed me to feel anger at him later on. All the rest of it, I said to myself, "Oh, he just slipped accidentally." But this was clearly thought out ahead of time. It was the only time he did anything that no one else saw him do. The rest of it was all out in the open.

I Didn't Know How to Say No

Before he molested me, I was a happy child. But after it happened, I started hanging out with guys with motorcycles, the kind of guys who drank a lot, had tattoos, and dropped out of school. I had a boyfriend who was a year older than me. I got pregnant the first time we had sex.

I was thirteen. I was afraid to tell my parents. I wore a lot of baggy clothes. I was six months pregnant before they figured it out. It shows how little parenting was going on.

My mother and I went shopping for a new bra because my breasts were swelling. When she saw me nude in the dressing room, she knew, but she didn't say anything to me. She came home and told my father. That night, when I was in bed, he came into my room and asked if I was pregnant. I said I was. He told me my mother had known I was pregnant because my breasts had changed, that the nipples were larger and the brown area around the nipples had gotten bigger and browner. Then he said he wanted to see. I protested. He said he wouldn't touch me, and he insisted that I pull up my shirt. He stared at my breasts for a few minutes, and then he let me pull my shirt down. I felt invaded and ashamed.

My parents never got angry at me for the pregnancy. They asked me what I wanted to do. I said I wanted to get rid of it. I flew to New York with my mother to some sleazy hospital for a saline abortion. The nurses had me give birth in a bedpan. It was only then that I realized it was a baby. It wasn't just a thing. I never found out if it was a girl or a boy.

My mother visited me a couple of times, but she only sat there crying. I ended up feeling guilty that I'd caused her all this pain. I felt like a horrible person. Once we got home, it was never mentioned again.

Why Was I Having Panic Attacks?

I started having anxiety attacks when I was a teenager, but they got really bad when I was in my twenties. They were crippling. Adrenaline would rush through my whole system. My muscles would pump up, my arms would tighten, my whole body would start to sweat and shake. My vision would change. It's like looking at an overexposed photo.

The panic attacks happened most frequently in the car. I'd be driving on the freeway and I'd feel like I was being forced to go faster than I wanted to go. When I had to pull up at a stop light, I'd feel completely trapped. I'd want to run the red light.

One of my sisters is an alcoholic. When I was twenty-five, she got into AA and started reading books about incest. She came to me and said, "What Dad did to us was incest."

I said, "Maybe for you, but not for me. I love my father. He loves me. He never did anything to hurt me."

It took the longest time for me to believe that my experience counted. I felt that what happened to me was so minor compared to other women. My father just slipped once in a while.

I think it was the panic attacks—the fact that there was a direct result I could point to—that made me start to believe that he had done something wrong. They pushed me to break through that barrier of protecting my father, to face how terrified and angry I had been.

I finally made the connection. It was like a suspense thriller where the girl has trusted someone to protect her from the killer, and all of a sudden, she finds out he *is* the killer. My father, who was supposed to keep me safe from harm, *was* the harm.

For the first time in my life, I got angry at my father. He lost his hero status.

At First I Felt Sorry for My Father

My sister confronted my father a couple of years ago. When she told me she'd talked to him, I felt sorry for him. All I could think was, "How is he going to handle it?" I'd taken care of my father's emotional needs for so long that it was hard for me to recognize that he was a sick person who did bad things.

My father's admitted to me that what he did was wrong. He says I'm still special to him, and that the only important thing is that I get better. For a while he'd call me. I'd get angry at him and he'd apologize. But it wasn't really helping me. Finally I told him I didn't want to do that anymore.

Recently I wrote him a letter and said I didn't want to have any contact with him for the time being. I was crying, but it felt terrific to write. It's hard because I don't know what kind of relationship I will have with my father when this is all over. I don't know what will be left. But at least I know I'm getting healthy.

For Supporters of Survivors

"We have a much more fulfilling and exciting relationship than the one we started with. It's made us close. I mean, you don't get close living in a bowl of cherries."

Being a close supporter of a survivor healing from child sexual abuse can be a tremendous challenge. Taking part in a deep healing process can lead to real growth and closeness. But you may also feel confused, scared, resentful, conflicted, isolated, or overwhelmed. You may not know what to say, what to feel, or how to act. These are natural responses to a difficult situation.

This is a time when it's important to take care of yourself. Honor your own needs. If the survivor wants you to give more than you're able to give, admit your limits. Encourage her to reach out to others. Take breaks.

Get help for yourself. Dealing with such raw pain

is difficult. You need a place you can go to talk about your own fears, doubts, and frustrations.

If you find yourself feeling extremely defensive or upset when the survivor talks about her abuse, it may be that you're reacting to experiences from your own past. This is common. One person's pain brings up hurt for another. If this is happening to you, seek help for dealing with your own unresolved pain.

How to Help

When a survivor tells you she was sexually abused, she is entrusting you with a part of her life that is painful, frightening, and vulnerable. These guidelines can help you honor that trust and help her healing:

- **Believe the survivor.** Even if her memories are unclear or too terrible to believe, believe her.
- **Join with the survivor in validating the damage.** All abuse is harmful. Even if it's not violent, physical, or repeated, all abuse has serious consequences.
- **Be clear that abuse is never the child's fault.** Children ask for attention and affection. They do not ask for sexual abuse. Even if a child responds sexually, wasn't forced, or didn't protest, it is still never the child's fault. It is always the responsibility of the adult not to be sexual with a child.
- **Educate yourself about sexual abuse and the healing process.**

- **Don't sympathize with the abuser.** The survivor needs your total loyalty.

- **Validate the survivor's feelings of anger, pain, and fear.** These are natural, healthy responses to abuse. She needs to feel them, express them, and be heard.

- **Express your feelings.** If you have feelings of outrage, sympathy, or pain, share them. Just make sure they don't overshadow the survivor's feelings.

- **Respect the time and space it takes to heal.** Healing is a slow process with lots of ups and downs. It can't be hurried.

- **Encourage the survivor to get help.** You can't be her only supporter.

- **Get help if the survivor is suicidal.** Don't hesitate or try to deal with it alone. Get professional help. If you don't know who else to call, ask the operator for the number for suicide prevention.

- **Accept that there will probably be changes in your relationship as the survivor heals.**

- **Resist seeing the survivor as a victim.** Continue to see her as a strong, courageous woman struggling to resolve a major trauma.

National Child Abuse Hotline

ChildHelp USA
1-800-422-4453

This free twenty-four-hour hotline offers crisis counseling, help in finding a counselor or support group in your area, and information for both adults and children who have been abused. They can also tell you how to report abuse.